Amelia & Alex Wasiliev
photography by Elisa Watson

 hachette
AUSTRALIA

CONTENTS

INTRODUCTION

What is Paleo?

The Paleo way of life has been around for a long time but only in the last couple of years have its benefits become more widely known and its lifestyle practiced.

The Paleo diet restricts processed foods, sugars, grains and dairy products and encourages a simple diet of fresh fruit and vegetables along with proteins, nuts and seeds.

Living the Paleo lifestyle is much more than a diet. It draws on the core values of the lifestyle of our historical ancestors who ate whole, unprocessed foods, who moved around more than we do, who slept better and had less stress. It is about having a conscious awareness of the food we eat and the effect it has on our body. It is also about making healthy choices in all areas of our life, so prioritising good sleeping habits, exercising regularly and working to reduce stress are all equally as important for optimum health.

Why eat Paleo?

This is a fairly simple question to answer. Eating Paleo means your diet and your body will be free of additives, preservatives, chemicals and unwanted toxins. You will be eating more fresh fruit and vegetables, which in turn increases the antioxidants and anti-inflammatory benefits to your body. You will be eating more red meats and proteins, which will increase the iron your body absorbs.

In essence you won't be eating anything that has bad properties. This means your body will be able to run efficiently, heal itself and function to its full potential.

Here are some of the main reported benefits of a Paleo lifestyle:

- improved gut health
- improved nutrient absorption
- weight loss
- muscle growth
- better sleep
- stabilised blood sugar (known to cure Type 2 diabetes)
- healthy skin
- increased brain function
- increased energy levels
- higher immune function
- reduced risk of heart disease and cancer
- reduced allergies.

WHAT SHOULD I EAT?

Foods to Avoid

 Sugar & artificial sweeteners

 Processed foods of any kind: *including ready meals & junk food*

 Grains and cereals of all kinds: *flour, rice, rye, barley, corn & oats*

 Legumes, beans, lentils, soy & peanuts

 Processed meats

 Processed vegetable oils

 Dairy products

 Potatoes: *high in starch and low in other nutrients*

 Soft drinks, energy drinks & alcohol

 Coffee: *caffeine stimulates your nervous system and can affect sleeping patterns and moods*

 Fruit juices

 Milk & white chocolate & sweets

Foods to Eat in Moderation

 Butter: *organic butter is accepted by most Paleo standards as a good inclusion as it is an animal fat. Eat only as your body allows*

 Salt: *limit your salt in cooking*

 Root vegetables: *sweet potato, beetroot, turnips and parsnips can all be eaten, however, they are high in carbohydrates and sugars. If trying Paleo to lose weight, eat them in moderation*

 Natural sweeteners: *maple syrup and raw honey are the best to use when eating a Paleo diet. Be aware that they are still very high in fructose and sucrose.*

 Dried fruit: *such as dates, apricots, sultanas, pineapple. Any dried fruit has a much higher fructose content than fresh. Only eat occasionally to avoid high sugar spikes and buy naturally dried products.*

 Sauces and dressings: *Nowadays a lot of your favourite sauces and dressings are made with a sugar-free alternative. Always check the labels. Make sure there are as few ingredients as possible and no added sugar.*

Foods to Eat & Embrace

 Meat & animal products: *beef, venison, lamb, duck and chicken. Unprocessed grass-fed meats from all animal types as well as animal products such as gelatine*

 Fish and seafood

 Fresh vegetables: *leafy greens, carrot, celery, kale, cauliflower, eggplant, onions, leeks, garlic, salad vegetables and herbs, such as parsley*

 Fresh fruits: *berries, apples, pears, avocados, the list goes on*

 Organic eggs

 Nuts: *almonds, cashews, pecans, hazelnuts and macadamia nuts. All nuts that are going to be eaten should be 'activated'. This process removes the enzyme inhibitors and allows the body to break them down more easily. You can buy nuts already activated or you can do it at home.*

To activate nuts: Put 150g nuts in a large bowl and pour in enough water to cover. Add 1 teaspoon salt and stir until the salt is dissolved. Soak for 12 hours, then drain, rinse and dry thoroughly.

 Seeds: *pumpkin seeds, sunflower, chia, flaxseed and sesame seeds.*

 Natural healthy oils: *olive oil, nut oil (except groundnut/peanut as it's a legume), avocado oil, sesame oil and fruit oils*

 Coconut oil: *a rich source of healthy, saturated fatty acids that is good to include on the Paleo diet.*

 Animal fats, lard & ghee: *great alternatives to vegetable oils when needed. They will fry at higher temperatures and there is no need to feel guilty about eating them*

 Coconut milk & cream: *great as a dairy alternative and can be used in smoothies, sweets and curries*

 Fermented foods: *excellent for your body's digestion as they contain natural healthy bacteria to aid digestion. Always make sure that there is no added sugar. The healthiest are lacto-fermented products, which are usually just fermented in salty water, such as the* Mixed pickled vegetables *(p.70)*

 Sea vegetables: *dulse, nori and wakame*

 Flour alternatives: *coconut flour, ground almonds, tapioca flour, arrowroot and chai seed flour are great alternatives to grain flours*

 Vinegars: *avoid malt and barley vinegars as they contain gluten, but those which are fermented and made with fruit are fine, such as apple cider vinegar, red and white wine vinegars and balsamic*

HOW TO START YOUR PALEO LIFESTYLE

It doesn't take much to begin the Paleo way of life. Clean out your fridge and pantry and spend an afternoon preparing some of the basic recipes in this book. If you need a little more inspiration, use the following menu plans to create your weekly shopping list. One thing is for sure, you won't be hungry! The Paleo lifestyle does not limit the amount of food you can eat so choose a couple of snacks in each day if you need it. After the first week, you will find that if you eat well at mealtimes you probably won't need snacks anyway.

MENU PLAN: WEEK 1

DAY 1:
Breakfast: *Scrambled eggs with bacon (p.52)*
Lunch: *Roasted beetroot & rocket salad (p.92)*
Dinner: *Bangers & sweet potato mash (p.128)*
with *Chinese broccoli with almonds (p.102)*
Snacks: *Fresh fruit, guacamole (p.76)*
with *Chia seed crackers (p.62)*

DAY 2:
Breakfast: *Almond milk banana smoothie (p.46)*
Lunch: Leftover *Chinese broccoli with
almonds (p.102)* and *Chorizo balls (p.68)*
Dinner: *Mediterranean lamb (p.130)*
Snacks: *Spiced nuts (p.64), Chopped raw
vegetables, (carrots, celery, cucumber)*

DAY 3:
Breakfast: *Breakfast waffles (p.48)*
Lunch: Leftover *Mediterranean lamb (p.130)*
with fresh rocket or spinach
Dinner: *Wild fish with salsa verde (p.144)*
Snacks: *Nut energy bars (p.152),*
Leftover *Chorizo balls (p.68)*

DAY 4:
Breakfast: *Bacon & egg breakfast cups (p.44)*
Lunch: *Chicken coleslaw (p.100)*
Dinner: *Caveman burger (p.118)*
Snacks: *Fresh fruit, Nut energy bars (p.152)*

DAY 5:
Breakfast: *Green smoothie (p.42)*
Lunch: *Zucchini fritters (p.66)* with
Brussels sprouts with bacon (p.90)
Dinner: *Paleo lasagne (p.134)*
Dessert: *Roasted peach crumble (p.156)*
Snack: *Bacon & egg breakfast cups (p.44)*

DAY 6: LEFTOVERS DAY
Breakfast: Leftover *Roasted peach
crumble (p.156)*
Lunch: Leftover *Paleo lasagne (p.134)*
Dinner: Leftover *Zucchini fritters (p.66)* with
Green salad with tahini dressing (p.86)
Snacks: *Nut energy bars (p.152),
Chia seed crackers (p.62)*

DAY 7:
Breakfast: *Egg with kale & eggplant hash (p.38)*
Lunch: *Buffalo wings (p.60)* with *Spring
onion carrot noodles (p.84)*
Dinner: *Mushroom & leek soup (p.140)*
Snack: *Spiced nuts (p.64), Fresh fruit*

MENU PLAN: WEEK 2

DAY 1:
Breakfast: *Blueberry chia pudding (p.40)*
Lunch: *Paleo bread (p.22) open sandwich (choose your own toppings my favourites include avocado, smoked fish, tomatoes and fresh herbs)* with leftover *Mushroom & leek soup (p.140)*
Dinner: *Scallops with parsnip purée (p.108)* and leftover *Spring onion carrot noodles (p.84)*
Snacks: *Sweet potato & sumac fries (p.96)*

DAY 2:
Breakfast: *Apple cinnamon French toast (p.56)*
Lunch: *Whole roasted mushrooms (p.98)* with *Pumpkin with nut cheese (p.88)*
Dinner: *Rib steaks with minty peas (p.122)*
Snack: *Baba ganoush (p.78) with raw chopped vegetables*

DAY 3:
Breakfast: *Breakfast omelette (p.50)*
Lunch: *Duck salad Asian style (p.94)*
Dinner: *Whole baked snapper (p.110)* with *Honey-roasted baby carrots (p.82)*
Snack: *Chia seed crackers (p.62)* with *Nut cheese (p.30)*

DAY 4:
Breakfast: *Green smoothie (p.42)*
Lunch: Leftover *Snapper (p.110)* with *Baba ganoush (p.78)* on *Paleo bread (p.22)*
Dinner: *Zucchini bolognese (p.132)*
Snack: *Nut energy bars (p.152)*

DAY 5:
Breakfast: *Egg with soldiers (p.54)*
Lunch: Leftover *Zucchini bolognese (p.132)*
Dinner: *Poule au pot (p.114)*
Dessert: *Paleo chocolate brownie (p.150)*
Snack: *Nutty raspberry friand bites (p.148)*

DAY 6: LEFTOVERS DAY
Breakfast: Leftover *Paleo bread (p.22)* with your choice of topping *(pure nut butters are a good breakfast option)*
Lunch: Leftover *Poule au pot (p.114)*
Dinner: *Sashimi salad (p.104)*
Snack: *Paleo chocolate brownie (p.150)*

DAY 7:
Breakfast: *Egg with kale & eggplant hash (p.38)*
Lunch: *Cauliflower fried rice (p.124)*
Dinner: *Pumpkin gnocchi (p.142)*
Snack: *Spiced nuts (p.64)*

Using leftovers

I try to allow for using leftovers in the next day's meals. Once a week have a leftovers day and give yourself a break from cooking. Don't forget you can add as much fresh fruit, vegetables, nuts and seeds to your daily intake as you need.

Note to dieters

If you have chosen to use the Paleo lifestyle as a way to lose weight (which you undoubtably will) it is best to limit your intake of high fructose fruits. Fresh fruits such as grapes, pineapples, apples, bananas, cherries and pears are high in fructose and although it is natural sugar it will still play havoc with your body's sugar levels. If losing weight is a priority then try to eat less dried fruits and root vegetables.

BASICS

Make these recipes in large quantities and keep on hand to add flavour and extra goodness to your Paleo diet. These basics will also help you to convert your usual favourite recipes to a Paleo-friendly version.

Chicken stock • Simple salad vinaigrette
Creamy tahini dressing • BBQ sauce
Paleo bread • Chilli sambal • Paleo tomato sauce
Paleo mayo • Nut cheese • Paleo onion jam
Cauliflower white sauce

CHICKEN STOCK

Makes: about 2 litres

YOU NEED

1 whole free-range chicken (can be swapped for other meats or fish for different stocks) • 2 brown onions, unpeeled and roughly chopped
2 celery sticks, roughly chopped • 1 garlic bulb, unpeeled and cut through the centre • 2 medium carrots, roughly chopped • 2 rosemary sprigs
2 thyme sprigs • 1 tablespoon coconut oil or olive oil • salt

This nutritious stock is high in vitamin B, zinc, phosphorus and
protein to help strengthen bones and teeth.

HR *Hair repairing*   **IF** *Infection fighting*   **A** *Anti-inflammatory*

In a large pan, heat vegetables, herbs, half the oil and seasoning over medium heat
for 7–10 minutes until browned. Make a well in centre. Rub remaining oil and salt
over chicken then place, skin side down, in the centre. Cook until caramelised. Pour
in enough water to cover the chicken. Bring to the boil. Cover and simmer for
2 hours, skimming scum from the top. Strain. Reserve liquid.

SIMPLE SALAD VINAIGRETTE

Makes: about 250ml

YOU NEED

150ml olive oil or your oil of choice (macadamia or avocado)

3 tablespoons apple cider vinegar • juice of ½ lemon

1 teaspoon wholegrain mustard • salt and freshly ground black pepper

Rich in monounsaturated fats and high in fibre to help balance blood sugar levels.

D *Aids digestion*   **HP** *Heart protection*   **A** *Anti-inflammatory*

Combine all ingredients in a jar with a screw-top lid. Shake well to combine. Taste and adjust as needed. Store in refrigerator for up to 2 weeks.

CREAMY TAHINI DRESSING

Makes: about 250ml

YOU NEED

100ml tahini paste • 100ml water • juice of 2 large lemons
1 garlic clove, finely diced • 2 handfuls of baby spinach leaves (flat-leaf parsley, basil
or dill are also good) • salt and freshly ground black pepper

A great source of calcium, magnesium and phosphorus, which helps to
strengthen bones and keep skin healthy.

E *Energy boosting*   **Hs** *Heart support*   **BP** *Blood pressure lowering*

Process all ingredients in a blender or food processor until smooth. Taste and add
more seasoning or lemon juice, if necessary. Add more water to achieve desired
consistency. Transfer to a jar and chill for up to 2 weeks.

BBQ SAUCE

Makes: about 250ml

YOU NEED

125ml *Paleo tomato sauce* (see page 26) • 1 small brown onion, diced
½ tablespoon chilli flakes • 60ml maple syrup • 1 small eggplant, cubed
½ red capsicum, diced • 1 tablespoon balsamic vinegar
½ tablespoon coconut oil • salt

The eggplant is high in fibre, low in calories and a good source of B vitamins while the onion contains sulphur, which is good for a healthy heart.

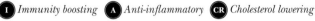

I *Immunity boosting*   **A** *Anti-inflammatory*   **CR** *Cholesterol lowering*

Preheat oven to 180°C/350°F/Gas 4. Toss eggplant, red capsicum and onion in oil and sprinkle with chilli flakes. Pour in maple syrup and vinegar. Season and cook for 30 minutes until roasted. Cool. Blitz ketchup with roasted ingredients in a food processor or blender until smooth. Add water if necessary to loosen. Strain to achieve a finer texture, if desired.

PALEO BREAD

Makes: 1 small loaf

YOU NEED

4 tablespoons coconut flour • 120g ground almonds • 2 tablespoons chia seeds, plus
extra for topping • 2 tablespoons sesame seeds, plus extra for topping
1 teaspoon bicarbonate of soda • 4 tablespoons LSA (ground linseeds, sunflower
seeds, almonds) • 1 zucchini, grated • 5 organic eggs
4 tablespoons coconut oil • 1 tablespoon apple cider vinegar

Full of fibre and helps to keep the brain and heart healthy.

BSt *Bone strengthening*   **EP** *Eye protection*   **CR** *Cholesterol lowering*

Preheat oven to 160°C/325°F/Gas 3. Grease and line a small 10 x 22cm loaf tin with baking paper. Combine all ingredients in bowl – it will form a runny batter. Transfer to tin, smooth top and sprinkle with mixture of sesame and chia seeds. Bake for 40–45 minutes until a skewer inserted into centre comes out clean. Remove from tin and serve. Store in airtight container for 4–5 days.

CHILLI SAMBAL

Makes: 150ml

YOU NEED

5 fresh cayenne chillies, diced • 20g garlic cloves, finely sliced
60ml red wine vinegar • ½ teaspoon salt • 1 lemongrass stalk, crushed
juice of 1 lime • 15g piece ginger, peeled and finely diced • 1 teaspoon sesame oil

Chilli can help to boost metabolism, improve digestion, help to clear
sinus congestion and may be able to relieve joint pain.

A *Anti-inflammatory*   **I** *Immunising*   **CR** *Cholesterol reducing*

Heat oil in pan over high heat. Add chillies, garlic, ginger, lemongrass and salt and
stir to combine. Pour in vinegar and lime juice. Once simmering, lower heat and
cook for 15–20 minutes until liquid has reduced. Cool. Store in an airtight jar or
blend to a more sauce-like consistency. Store for up to 2 weeks.

PALEO TOMATO SAUCE

Makes: about 250ml

YOU NEED

4–5 shallots • 3 large garlic cloves, peeled • 3 ripe tomatoes • 250ml passata
60ml red wine vinegar • 1 handful of parsley, chopped • 250ml water • salt

Tomatoes are full of antioxidants, beta-carotene and vitamin C to help keep the cardiovascular system healthy.

BSt *Bone strengthening*   **D** *Aids digestion*   **BP** *Blood pressure lowering*

Preheat oven to 200°C/400°F/Gas 6. Combine tomatoes, garlic and shallots in baking dish. Add oil, vinegar and a pinch of salt and bake for 15 minutes until shallots and garlic have softened and vinegar reduced. Blitz in food processer or blender with passata and water until smooth. Season to taste. Pour into pan, add parsley and simmer for 20–25 minutes. Either strain or keep chunky. Cool before chilling for 2–3 weeks.

PALEO MAYO

Makes: about 250ml

YOU NEED
3 organic egg yolks • 250ml light tasting olive oil
1 spring onion, finely diced • 1 small garlic clove, finely diced
1 teaspoon Dijon mustard • ½ teaspoon red wine vinegar
½ teaspoon raw honey • salt • lemon juice (optional)

Rich in vitamins A and D to help keep the eyes healthy and improve night vision.

A *Anti-inflammatory*   **Hs** *Heart support*   **BSt** *Bone strengthening*

Combine egg yolks, spring onions, garlic, mustard and honey and process on medium speed in a food processor for 1 minute. Combine oils in a jug and while food processor is on slowly drizzle in oil, a little at a time, allowing ingredients to emulsify until it is a thick, creamy consistency. Add salt, vinegar and lemon juice to taste. Chill in an airtight jar for 2 weeks.

NUT CHEESE

Makes: about 200g

YOU NEED
150g cashew nuts • 2 garlic cloves, roasted • juice of 1 lemon
1 bunch of chives, finely chopped • 1 teaspoon sea salt

Cashews are packed with monounsaturated fats to keep the heart
healthy and help to lower cholesterol.

S *Skin repairing*   **E** *Energisng*   **BSt** *Bone strengthening*

Soak cashews in water for 2–3 hours. Drain, rinse well and rub dry with kitchen
paper. Put in food processor, add remaining ingredients, except chives, and blend
well to a grainy paste. Transfer to bowl or round mould, cover and chill for
1–2 hours until set. Remove from mould and roll edges in chives to serve.
Chill for 4–5 days.

PALEO ONION JAM

Makes: about 250ml

YOU NEED

2 large Spanish onions, cut into thin rings

3 tablespoons sugar-free strawberry jam • 2 tablespoons organic butter

2 tablespoons red wine vinegar • 2 tablespoons coconut oil • salt

Red onions are a good source of vitamin C and can help to regulate blood sugar levels as well as lower blood pressure.

AF *Anti-fungal*　**A** *Anti-inflammatory*　**HP** *Heart protection*

Put pan over low heat, add oil and butter and let butter melt. Add onions and cook for 10 minutes until softened and glassy looking. Season with salt and stir through. Add vinegar and jam and cook, stirring for 10–15 minutes until onions soften and thicken. Cool and keep chilled for up to 2 weeks.

CAULIFLOWER WHITE SAUCE

Makes: about 375ml

YOU NEED
½ cauliflower, roughly chopped • 3 basil sprigs with leaves

2 garlic cloves, roughly chopped • 2 small shallots, roughly chopped

80g ghee • 500ml *Chicken stock* (see page 14)

2 tablespoons olive oil • salt

Cauliflower contains lots of vitamins C and K to help keep the cardiovascular system healthy.

De *Detoxifying*   **A** *Anti-inflammatory*   **D** *Aids digestion*

Heat oil in a pan over medium heat. Cook shallots, garlic and one-third of ghee for 7 minutes until softened. Add cauliflower, season and cook for 4–5 minutes until cauliflower has browned. Add stock and basil. Cover, bring to the boil. Simmer for 10–15 minutes. Remove basil, strain liquid and discard. Blitz cauliflower mix with remaining ghee and pinch of salt in a food processor until smooth.

BREAKFAST & BRUNCH

*Who doesn't love a cooked breakfast every day?
The Paleo lifestyle is excellent for the cooked
breakfast lover – simple eggs and bacon or you
can be more creative. Most of your favourites
can be converted to be Paleo friendly and if you
are short on time in the morning, try a quick
and easy delicious smoothie.*

Egg with kale & eggplant hash
Blueberry chia pudding • Green smoothie
Bacon & egg breakfast cups • Almond milk
banana smoothie • Breakfast waffles • Breakfast
omelette • Scrambled eggs with bacon • Eggs
with soldiers • Apple cinnamon French toast

EGG WITH KALE & EGGPLANT HASH

Serves: 1

YOU NEED

2 stalks of curly kale, leaves finely shredded • 1 baby eggplant, diced
½ zucchini, diced • ½ shallot, finely diced • 1 tablespoon apple cider vinegar
1½ tablespoons pine nuts, toasted • 1 organic egg • ½ tablespoon coconut oil • salt

Rich in antioxidants and calcium to help keep the joints and cartilage healthy.

BSt *Bone strengthening*   **A** *Anti-inflammatory*   **De** *Detoxifying*

Toast pine nuts in dry frying pan over medium heat for a few minutes. Set aside.
Heat oil in pan and sauté shallots for 5 minutes. Add eggplant, zucchini and season
to taste. Cook, stirring until vegetables brown. Add kale and vinegar and cook for
2–3 minutes. Put hash onto plate. Fry egg, put on top of hash,
then sprinkle with pine nuts.

BLUEBERRY CHIA PUDDING

Serves: 2

YOU NEED

2 tablespoons chia seeds • 100ml coconut milk (or any nut milk)
1 tablespoon maple syrup (optional) • 1 vanilla pod, split in half lengthways and
seeds scraped out • 2 teaspoons toasted pumpkin seeds
2 tablespoons water • 2 small handfuls of fresh blueberries

Blueberries are high in fibre and vitamin E to reduce the risk of heart disease and help maintain healthy blood pressure.

Bs *Blood sugar stabilising*   **EP** *Eye protecting*   **CR** *Cholesterol reducing*

Whisk together coconut milk, chia seeds, vanilla seeds and maple syrup, if using. Set aside for 5 minutes then whisk to make sure the chia seeds are dispersed. Add a handful of berries and mix well. Put into small bowls, cover and chill for 2 hours, or until set. Top with remaining berries and pumpkin seeds. Chill for up to 4 days.

GREEN SMOOTHIE

Makes: 250ml

YOU NEED

½ avocado • 2 stalks of curly kale, leaves removed • 2 handfuls of baby spinach
150g fresh or frozen pineapple • 1 orange, peeled • 60ml coconut cream

Dark leafy greens are rich in vitamins C, A and K as well as calcium, potassium and folate and can help boost the immune system.

A *Anti-inflammatory* **De** *Detoxifying* **Hs** *Heart support*

Blend all ingredients in a blender until smooth. Add 60–120ml water depending on desired consistency and blend until combined. Serve immediately.

BACON & EGG BREAKFAST CUPS

Makes: 8

YOU NEED

8 rashers of streaky grass-fed bacon • 8 organic eggs • 1 teaspoon chilli flakes
1 teaspoon black sesame seeds • coconut oil or butter, for greasing
2 spring onions, finely sliced • salt and freshly ground black pepper

Bacon is packed with choline to help with memory and vitamin B12, which is important for keeping red blood cells healthy.

E *Energising* **BB** *Brain boosting* **BSt** *Bone strengthening*

Preheat oven to 200°C/400°F/Gas 6. Grease 12-hole muffin tin. Use bacon to line base and sides of tin then bake for 10–15 minutes until it starts to brown and crisp. In a bowl, combine chilli flakes, sesame seeds and a pinch of salt and pepper. Break egg into each bacon-lined hole. Sprinkle with chilli mixture and bake for 7–8 minutes until yolk is cooked to your preference. Serve or chill for up to 4 days.

ALMOND MILK BANANA SMOOTHIE

Makes: 250ml

YOU NEED

150ml almond milk • 1 banana • 2 pitted Medjool dates • 1 tablespoon honey

High in calcium, potassium and vitamin E and low in fat to help build strong
muscles and keep the heart healthy.

BSt *Bone strengthening*   **S** *Skin repairing*   **BP** *Blood pressure reducing*

Blend all ingredients in a blender until smooth, adding water to thin to desired
consistency, if necessary. Serve immediately.

BREAKFAST WAFFLES

Makes: 6–8

YOU NEED

3 organic eggs, lightly beaten • 150ml almond milk • 75g organic butter, melted,
plus extra for greasing • 180g ground almonds • 3 tablespoons coconut flour
3 tablespoons tapioca flour • 1½ tablespoons baking powder • 1 banana, sliced
1 handful of toasted chopped nuts

High in fibre and promotes heart health including helping to maintain normal blood pressure.

S *Skin repairing* **D** *Aids digestion* **E** *Energising*

Melt butter and combine with all dry ingredients in a bowl. In a jug, combine remaining wet ingredients. Pour wet ingredients into dry and stir. Rest for 20 minutes, then pour in 80ml water and stir to loosen. Heat waffle iron or griddle pan and cook each waffle for 6–7 minutes until golden brown and crisp. Top with banana and nuts.

BREAKFAST OMELETTE

Serves: 1

YOU NEED

3 organic eggs • 50ml coconut cream

100g hot smoked salmon, torn into bite-sized pieces

1 tablespoon capers • 10g flat-leaf parsley, finely chopped

2 spring onions, sliced • 1 tablespoon coconut oil or olive oil

This omelette is full of good fats and helps to strengthen the immune system and keep the brain healthy.

Hs *Heart support*   **EP** *Eye protecting*   **Mm** *Aids memory*

Beat eggs, coconut cream and 20ml water together. Add parsley, spring onions and salmon and mix well. Heat oil in frying pan over medium heat. Pour in egg mixture and let egg begin to set. Sprinkle capers over top, then move egg around to let it cook and set all over. When top is set, flip one side of omelette onto other and serve immediately.

SCRAMBLED EGGS WITH BACON

Serves: 1

YOU NEED

6–8 cherry tomatoes on vine • 1 rasher of grass-fed bacon, cut in half

2 organic eggs • ½ tablespoon coconut oil • salt

Chilli sambal (see page 24), optional

High in protein and rich in antioxidants, vitamin B and choline,
which is important for keeping cells healthy.

BSt *Bone strengthening*   **E** *Energising*   **BB** *Brain boosting*

Preheat oven to 200°C/400°F/Gas 6. Place bacon in baking dish and bake for
10 minutes. Turn bacon over and add tomatoes. Bake for 5–10 minutes. Whisk eggs
and 20ml water together. Heat oil in frying pan over low heat. Add eggs, season and
cook slowly to your liking. Serve with bacon, tomatoes and chilli sambal, if using.

EGGS WITH SOLDIERS

Serves: 1

YOU NEED
2 organic eggs • 6–8 asparagus stalks, trimmed • avocado oil, for drizzling
salt and freshly ground black pepper

Asparagus is packed with vitamins A, C, E and K and is a good source of fibre to help protect against heart disease and boost the immune system.

A *Anti-inflammatory* **BB** *Brain boosting* **BSt** *Bone strengthening*

Bring a full small pan of water to the boil. Carefully place eggs into the water and cook for 5 minutes. Remove from pan with a slotted spoon and run under cold water. Drop asparagus into the boiling water for 1–2 minutes. Drain, drizzle with oil and season. Peel or cut the top off eggs and serve with asparagus.

APPLE CINNAMON FRENCH TOAST

Serves: 1

YOU NEED

1 green apple, peeled and thinly sliced • ½ teaspoon ground cinnamon

2 slices of *Paleo bread* (see page 22) • 1 organic egg, lightly beaten

20g organic butter • maple syrup (optional)

High in antioxidants and fibre and can help to lower cholesterol.

HP *Heart protection*   **BB** *Brain boosting*   **Bs** *Blood sugar stabilising*

Heat apples and half the butter in a pan over low heat for 4–5 minutes until apple is golden and soft. Add cinnamon and cook, stirring, for 1–2 minutes. Heat remaining butter in frying pan. Dip bread slices in egg to lightly coat, then fry for 2 minutes on each side until egg is set and golden. Fry second slice. Serve with apples drizzled with maple syrup, if using.

FINGER FOOD

Don't get confused and think this is a diet book. The Paleo lifestyle in no way limits the amount of food you can eat and there is no need to feel hungry. Make sure you have a constant supply of these quick Paleo snacks to keep your appetite in check.

Buffalo wings • Chia seed crackers • Spiced nuts
Zucchini fritters • Chorizo balls
Mixed pickled vegetables • Chilli salt squid
Fresh oysters • Guacamole • Baba ganoush

BUFFALO WINGS

Serves: 2

YOU NEED

400g chicken wings • 125ml *BBQ sauce* (see page 20)
1 tablespoon nutritional yeast flakes • 1 teaspoon allspice
1 teaspoon smoked paprika • ½ tablespoon coconut oil

High in protein, B vitamins, phosphorous, calcium and zinc to help strengthen bones and teeth.

BP *Blood pressure lowering* **MB** *Muscle building* **Hs** *Heart support*

Preheat oven to 200°C/400°F/Gas 6. Cut chicken wings into 3. Discard spikey wing tip. Oil roasting dish and toss wings around. Roast for 30–40 minutes until golden brown and skin is starting to crisp. Combine sauce with remaining ingredients. Remove wings from oven and toss through sauce mixture to evenly coat. Serve.

CHIA SEED CRACKERS

Makes: about 20 crackers

YOU NEED

50g LSA (ground linseed, sunflower seeds and almonds) • 65g sesame seeds
65g chia seeds • 60g pumpkin seeds • 2 teaspoons tamari
3 teaspoons seaweed flakes • 1 tablespoon nutritional yeast flakes • 225ml water

*It is best to use activated nuts and seeds if you can.

A good source of iodine and fibre and contains anti-inflammatory properties.

T *Thyroid regulating*　　**G** *Gluten-free*　　**CR** *Cholesterol reducing*

Preheat oven to 160°C/325°F/Gas 3. Line baking tray with baking paper. Combine dry ingredients, stirring to mix. Mix water and tamari then pour into dry ingredients and mix well. Rest for 5–10 minutes. Mix again and spread out over baking tray. Press down with back of spoon to smooth and push to 5mm thick. Bake for 30 minutes. Cut into even cracker shapes, turn crackers over and bake for 20–25 minutes until crisp. Cool and store in airtight container for 7–10 days.

SPICED NUTS

Makes 300g

YOU NEED

100g activated almonds • 100g activated cashew nuts
100g activated macadamia nuts • 2 tablespoons coconut oil
½ tablespoon dried garlic granules • 1 teaspoon chilli flakes
1 teaspoon sweet paprika • ½ tablespoon sea salt flakes

Nuts are packed with protein, essential fats, vitamin E and zinc to help keep the skin healthy, soft and supple.

SP *Skin Protection* **A** *Anti-inflammatory* **Hs** *Heart support*

Preheat oven to 200°C/400°F/Gas 6. Melt oil in roasting dish in oven for 1–2 minutes. Add nuts and toss to coat in oil. Roast for 10–12 minutes, tossing once. Meanwhile, combine remaining ingredients. Remove nuts from oven and toss spice mix through them. Cool then serve or store in an airtight container for a week.

ZUCCHINI FRITTERS

Makes: 8–10

YOU NEED

2 medium zucchini, grated • 2 tablespoons coconut flour
2 tablespoons tapioca flour • 2 spring onions, thinly sliced
15g coriander sprigs, chopped • 1 organic egg, lightly beaten
1 teaspoon salt • 1 tablespoon coconut oil

Zucchini are full of fibre to help promote good bowel function and antioxidants to reduce the risk of strokes.

CR *Cholesterol reducing* **D** *Aids digestion* **HP** *Heart protection*

Combine all ingredients, except oil, in a bowl and stir well. Heat a portion of oil in a frying pan over medium heat. Use a large spoon to drop 3 heaped spoonfuls of mixture into the pan and cook for 2–3 minutes on each side until golden. Rest cooked fritters on kitchen paper and repeat with remaining batter. Serve warm.

CHORIZO BALLS

Makes: about 16 balls

YOU NEED

½ onion, finely diced • ½ red capsicum, finely diced
3 garlic cloves, finely diced • 350g grass-fed pork mince
4 teaspoons smoked paprika • 1 tablespoon red wine vinegar
4 tablespoons refined coconut oil • 1 handful of chopped flat-leaf parsley
lemon wedges, to serve • a pinch of salt

Chorizo is high in protein, which helps to boost the immune system.

E *Energising*   **Mm** *Aids Memory*   **G** *Gluten-free*

Heat half the oil in a pan over medium heat. Sauté onions, garlic and red capsicum for 4–5 minutes. Add paprika, vinegar and salt and stir. Put in bowl, add mince and stir well. Cover and chill for 2 hours, or overnight. Roll heaped tablespoon of mixture to form a ball. Continue with remaining mixture. In frying pan, heat remaining oil over medium heat and cook 4–5 balls at a time for 7–8 minutes until browned and cooked through. Garnish with parsley and lemon.

MIXED PICKLED VEGETABLES

Makes: 1 litre jar

YOU NEED

½ cauliflower, cut into small florets • 2 carrots, diagonally sliced
1 bunch of breakfast radishes, quartered • ½ red capsicum, sliced
3 garlic cloves, squashed • 2 jalapeño chillies, deseeded and quartered
1 bay leaf • ½ teaspoon whole black peppercorns • 3 tablespoons sea salt flakes

Promotes gut health due to the healthy bacteria and contains essential vitamins and minerals including vitamins A, C and K as well as iron and potassium.

 D *Aids digestion*   **G** *Gluten-free*   **W** *Weight loss*

Fill a clean 1 litre jar with vegetables, spices and herbs. In a bowl, mix salt into 875ml filtered water. Pour into jar to cover vegetables. Add more water if necessary. Make sure jar is tightly sealed and stand at room temperature for 2–5 days. Once a day open jar to release gas and to taste pickles. Scrape away any scum or mould then cover. When you are happy with the taste, chill. Store for up to 6–8 weeks.

CHILLI SALT SQUID

Serves: 4

YOU NEED

1 heaped teaspoon chilli flakes • 55g activated cashew nuts

40g coconut flour • 1 teaspoon salt • 400g cleaned squid tubes

2 organic eggs, beaten • 30g lard • lemon slices, to serve

Squid is high in protein and promotes good bone and teeth health.

I *Immunising*   **S** *Skin repairing*   **Bs** *Blood sugar stabilising*

Blitz chilli, cashews, flour and salt in a food processor until a fine breadcrumb-like texture. Spread on plate. Split squid lengthways down middle then into 4cm lengths. Heat lard in wok. Dip 1 piece of squid at a time in beaten egg then in crumb mixture to lightly coat. Fry for 2 minutes until golden brown. Drain on kitchen paper. Garnish with lemon.

FRESH OYSTERS

Serves: 4

YOU NEED
8–12 large fresh oysters, cleaned and opened • ½ cucumber, finely diced
juice of 1 lime • 1 shallot, finely diced • 2 tablespoons red wine vinegar • salt

Oysters are packed with zinc and some consider them to be powerful aphrodisiacs.

I *Immunising*   **Hs** *Heart support*   **M** *Metabolism boosting*

In a bowl, mix shallots and vinegar together. In another bowl, combine cucumber, lime juice and a sprinkle of salt. Place oysters on a platter (with ice if you want to keep them cold). Divide oysters and place 1 teaspoon of vinegar sauce on 1 half, and the cucumber-lime mix on the other.

GUACAMOLE

Serves: 4

YOU NEED

2 ripe avocados, peeled and pitted • 25g coriander leaves, finely chopped
2 shallots, finely diced • 2 red chillies, finely diced • juice of 1½ limes

Avocados are packed with heart-healthy fats to help keep the cardiovascular system strong as well as improve the skin to keep it soft and wrinkle free.

A *Anti-inflammatory*   **IF** *Infection fighting*   **BP** *Blood pressure lowering*

Mash avocado flesh in a bowl. Add remaining ingredients and mix well to combine. Serve immediately.

BABA GANOUSH

Serves: 4

YOU NEED

1 large eggplant • 2 garlic cloves, finely diced • 3 tablespoons tahini
juice of 1 lemon • ½ teaspoon smoked paprika • 10g flat-leaf parsley, finely chopped
1 tablespoon macadamia or olive oil • salt

High in fibre, B vitamins, potassium and magnesium
and can help with weight management.

Ⓐ *Anti-inflammatory*   ⒶⒶ *Anti-ageing*   ⒸⓇ *Cholesterol reducing*

Preheat oven to 180°C/350°F/Gas 4. Prick eggplant a few times with a fork and
char on flame of stove for a few minutes on each side until skin is blistering and
softening. Put into roasting dish and bake for 15–20 minutes until soft. Cool slightly
and remove skin. Blitz eggplant flesh with remaining ingredients and seasoning in a
food processor until desired consistency is reached. Serve.

SIDES & SALADS

These sides and salads can easily be a meal on their own but pair one or two dishes with some eggs, seafood or a quick seared steak and you have a simple and delicious feast.

Honey-roasted baby carrots • Spring onion carrot
noodles • Green salad with tahini dressing
Pumpkin with nut cheese
Brussels sprouts with bacon • Roasted beetroot
& rocket salad • Duck salad Asian style
Sweet potato & sumac fries • Whole roasted
mushrooms • Chicken coleslaw • Chinese
broccoli with almonds • Sashimi salad

HONEY-ROASTED BABY CARROTS

Serves: 2

YOU NEED
1 bunch of mixed baby carrots, peeled • 20g flat-leaf parsley, finely chopped
2 tablespoons honey • 1 tablespoon coconut or olive oil

50 minutes

Carrots are rich in vitamin A, which is good for vision, and also contain vitamin C to help boost the immune system.

D *Aids digestion*   **Hs** *Heart support*   **CR** *Cholesterol lowering*

Preheat oven to 180°C/350°F/Gas 4. In a pan combine the oil, honey and 15g parsley and heat to melt oil and honey. Arrange carrots in single layer in roasting dish. Pour honey mix over and toss to coat carrots evenly. Roast for 40 minutes, tossing once or twice. Top with remaining parsley to serve.

SPRING ONION CARROT NOODLES

Serves: 2

YOU NEED

3 large carrots, peeled • 1 small bunch of coriander

1 tablespoon grated ginger • 1 teaspoon chilli flakes

2 spring onions, thinly sliced • 1 tablespoon sesame oil

2 teaspoons honey • 1 tablespoon toasted sesame seeds

Carrots are high in fibre to aid good digestive health and spring onions contain sulphur to help control blood pressure.

CR *Cholesterol reducing*   **Ab** *Antibacterial*   **Hs** *Heart support*

Using a vegetable peeler or spiraliser, make noodles with carrots. Heat sesame oil in wok. Add ginger, spring onions and chilli flakes and sauté for 1 minute. Add carrots. Top with honey and cook, stirring, for 4 minutes. Carrots should still have bite. Top with coriander and sesame seeds and serve.

GREEN SALAD WITH TAHINI DRESSING

Serves: 1 as a main or 2–4 as a side

YOU NEED

100g mixed lettuce leaves • ½ avocado, peeled, pitted and sliced
½ medium cucumber, sliced • 1 handful of sugar snap peas, podded • 2 mint leaves,
roughly chopped • 30g pumpkin seeds, roasted • 1 handful of pea shoots
3 tablespoons *Creamy tahini dressing* (see page 18)

High in phytoestrogen and minerals to support the cardiovascular system and respiratory health.

BSt *Bone strengthening* **EP** *Eye protecting* **Hs** *Heart support*

Combine all green ingredients in a bowl. Pour dressing over and toss. Serve.
Top with pumpkin seeds.

PUMPKIN WITH NUT CHEESE

Serves: 4

YOU NEED

¼ pumpkin (any variety), cored and sliced • 1 teaspoon chilli flakes
2 teaspoons sea salt • 1 rosemary sprig, leaves removed and chopped
1 tablespoon coconut oil • 2–3 tablespoons *Nut cheese* (see page 30)

Pumpkins are high in fibre and low in calories to help with weight management, and also contain vitamin A to help with vision.

S *Skin repairing* **Hs** *Heart support* **CR** *Cholesterol reducing*

Preheat oven to 200°C/400°F/Gas 6. Mix salt, chilli and rosemary together. Rub pumpkin in oil and sprinkle with salt mix. Roast in oven for 15 minutes. Check and turn if needed, then roast for another 10 minutes until pumpkin is soft and browned. Crumble nut cheese over pumpkin and serve.

BRUSSELS SPROUTS WITH BACON

Serves: 4

YOU NEED
2 handfuls of Brussels sprouts • 1 rasher of grass-fed bacon, diced
20g activated pecan nuts • ½ tablespoon olive oil

Bacon and Brussels sprouts are packed with iron to help in the formation of red blood cells.

E *Energising*   **I** *Immunising*   **A** *Anti-inflammatory*

Steam Brussels sprouts over hot water for 4–5 minutes until just softening. Set aside. Toast pecans in dry frying pan for 4–5 minutes. Set aside. Cook bacon until browned and crisp, then add Brussels sprouts and pecans and toss together to coat in bacon flavour. Drizzle with olive oil, if needed and serve.

ROASTED BEETROOT & ROCKET SALAD

Serves: 1

YOU NEED

1 large beetroot, cut into eighths • 1 large handful of rocket

1 large handful of spinach • 2 tablespoons toasted sunflower seeds

2 tablespoons *Nut cheese* (see page 30)

2 tablespoons *Simple salad vinaigrette* (see page 16)

1 tablespoon coconut oil • salt and freshly ground black pepper

Beetroot is high in nitrates, which helps blood vessels to relax, while rocket has high levels of chlorophyll.

A *Anti-inflammatory* **De** *Detoxifying* **CR** *Cholesterol reducing*

Preheat oven to 200°C/400°F/Gas 6. Toss beetroot in oil and season. Place in baking dish and roast for 20–30 minutes until beetroot is soft when pricked with a fork. In last 5 minutes of roasting add sunflower seeds. In a bowl, combine remaining ingredients. Add beetroot and pine nuts and toss together to combine.

DUCK SALAD ASIAN STYLE

Serves: 1

YOU NEED

1 organic duck breast with skin on • 1 teaspoon Chinese five-spice powder

1 teaspoon salt • 1 carrot, julienned • 1 baby bok choy, roughly chopped

40g beansprouts • 20g mint and/or coriander leaves

½ tablespoon sesame oil • 1 teaspoon maple syrup

½ tablespoon fish sauce • juice of 1 lime

Duck is a good source of protein and is rich in vitamins and minerals, particularly selenium, which boosts the immune system, and bok choi, which is full of vitamins A, C and K.

SH *Skin & hair support*   **IF** *Infection fighting*   **BSt** *Bone strengthening*

Preheat oven to 180°C/350°F/Gas 4. Combine salt and five-spice powder and rub over duck skin. Heat oil in pan over high heat. Cook duck, skin side down, for 6–7 minutes until browned and crispy. Transfer to baking tray, skin side up, and cook in oven for 10 minutes. Rest for 5 minutes. Combine vegetables and herbs. Slice duck and add to vegetables. Whisk maple syrup, lime juice and fish sauce together. Pour over salad and toss to combine.

SWEET POTATO & SUMAC FRIES

Serves: 2

YOU NEED

1 tablespoon ghee or duck fat • 400–500g sweet potatoes, cut into chips

2 teaspoons sumac • salt to taste

Sweet potatoes are rich in beta-carotene, which helps to reduce the risk of heart disease and to fight off infections.

EP *Eye protecting*   **A** *Anti-inflammatory*   **Bs** *Blood sugar stabilising*

Preheat oven to 200°C/400°F/Gas 6. Toss sweet potatoes in duck fat, then arrange on baking tray, spaced apart. Sprinkle with sumac and salt and roast for about 30–40 minutes until soft in centre and golden brown. Turn halfway through roasting so evenly cooked. Serve hot.

WHOLE ROASTED MUSHROOMS

Serves: 2–4

YOU NEED

5–6 portobello mushrooms • 4 tablespoons *Chilli sambal* (see page 24)
2 rosemary sprigs, leaves removed • 1 tablespoon olive oil • salt to taste

Mushrooms contain vitamin D, calcium, potassium and are a good source of B vitamins to help strengthen the immune system and also promote weight loss.

(A) *Anti-inflammatory*   (Hs) *Heart support*   (BSt) *Bone strengthening*

Toss mushrooms with half the oil, chilli sambal, rosemary and a sprinkle of salt in an airtight container. Ensure that chilli is rubbed over mushrooms. Cover and marinate for 1–4 hours. Preheat oven to 180°C/350°F/Gas 4. Pour remaining oil in roasting dish. Spread out mushrooms, gill side up, leaving space between them and cook for 35–40 minutes until mushrooms are soft and juicy.

CHICKEN COLESLAW

Serves: 1

YOU NEED

1 free-range chicken breast, cooked and shredded • 150g red cabbage, shredded
5g mint, finely shredded • ½ small fennel, finely sliced
1 apple, peeled, cored and julienned • 2 tablespoons *Paleo mayo* (see page 28)
juice of ½ lemon • salt to taste

Packed with fibre and lots of essential vitamins and minerals including C, K, A and B vitamins.

I *Immunising* **EP** *Eye protecting* **Hs** *Heart support*

Whisk mayo and lemon juice together, adding 1–2 tablespoons water, if needed to thin dressing consistency. Season with a pinch of salt. Combine remaining ingredients in another bowl. Pour dressing over and toss to combine well.

CHINESE BROCCOLI WITH ALMONDS

Serves: 2–4

YOU NEED

1 bunch of Chinese broccoli, chopped into 5–7.5cm pieces

80g activated almonds • 2 teaspoons sesame oil • 1 tablespoon tamari

5g piece ginger, peeled and freshly grated • 1 teaspoon chilli flakes

Promotes heart health, helps to lower cholesterol and keeps the skin healthy.

I *Immunisng*　**E** *Energising*　**BSt** *Bone strengthening*

Toast almonds in dry frying pan over medium heat. Set aside. Heat oil and ginger
in pan then add broccoli. Toss to coat in oil then pour over tamari and chilli flakes.
Keep stirring and moving to let thicker parts of stem cook. After broccoli is well
coated add 1 tablespoon water, cover and steam for 1–2 minutes until cooked.
Uncover, sprinkle with almonds and chilli, stir and cook for 1–2 minutes.

SASHIMI SALAD

Serves: 1

YOU NEED

1 handful of watercress • 1 handful of frisee lettuce

200g fresh sushi-grade tuna, sliced • 2 teaspoons black sesame seeds

3 good-sized radishes, shaved • 2 tablespoons tamari

a sprinkle of seaweed flakes • juice of 1 lemon

Watercress is a rich source of vitamin K, calcium and manganese to keep teeth strong while tuna contains plenty of healthy omega-3 fats.

I *Immunising* · **Hs** *Heart support* · **BSt** *Bone strengthening*

Whisk tamari, lemon juice and seaweed flakes together in a bowl. Set aside. Arrange lettuce and watercress out on a plate, top with tuna slices and sprinkle with radishes and sesame seeds. Pour over dressing and serve.

MEALS

All of these recipes can be doubled or tripled to make larger quantities if necessary. I suggest always having extra cooked meats on hand for snacks or to add to fresh or cooked vegetables for a new dish altogether.

Scallops with parsnip purée
Whole baked snapper • Beef bourguignon
Poule au pot • Pot au feu • Caveman burger
Garlic & chilli prawns • Rib steaks with minty peas
Cauliflower fried rice • Pork & pears
Bangers & sweet potato mash • Mediterranean
lamb • Zucchini bolognese • Paleo lasagne
Seafood chowder • Vegetable curry
Mushroom & leek soup • Pumpkin gnocchi
Wild fish with salsa verde

SCALLOPS WITH PARSNIP PURÉE

Serves: 2

YOU NEED

375ml *Chicken stock* (see page 14) • 2 small parsnips, roughly chopped
1 shallot, diced • 1 small handful of pea shoots • 1 lemon
4 large fresh sea scallops • 2 tablespoons coconut oil
1 tablespoon butter (optional) • salt to taste

Full of protein, B vitamins, vitamin C and potassium to keep the heart healthy.

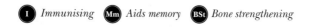

I *Immunising*   **Mm** *Aids memory*   **BSt** *Bone strengthening*

Heat 1 tablespoon oil in lidded pan. Brown shallots and parsnips. Season and add stock. Cover and cook for 30 minutes until parsnips are soft. Strain liquid and reserve. Blend parsnips and shallots in food processor, adding some reserved liquid until smooth, then strain. Heat remaining oil and butter, if using, in pan until bubbling. Add scallops, season and cook for 3 minutes each side. Serve over purée with pea shoots and lemon juice.

WHOLE BAKED SNAPPER

Serves: 1–2

YOU NEED

1 whole snapper, cleaned and gutted • 30g flat-leaf parsley

10g thyme, leaves picked • 2 lemons, 1 sliced, the other juiced

1 large leek, thinly sliced in half rounds • 2 shallots, finely diced

20g organic butter • 1 tablespoon coconut oil • salt to taste

Rich in omega-3 fatty acids and selenium to help improve brain function.

 Immunising **EP** *Eye protecting* **HP** *Heart protection*

Preheat oven to 180°C/350°F/Gas 4. Stuff fish with lemon slices, parsley and thyme.
Rub both sides of fish with half the oil and salt. Heat remaining oil in pan over high-
medium heat. Cook fish for 2 minutes on each side. Put in roasting dish and bake
for 10 minutes. Heat butter in same pan. Add shallots and leeks and cook for
6–8 minutes until leeks are soft. Add lemon juice and cook for 5 minutes.
Serve fish on top of leeks.

BEEF BOURGUIGNON

Serves: 4

YOU NEED

800g grass-fed shoulder steak, cut into large cubes • 2 celery sticks, diced
2 leeks, finely sliced • 2 tablespoons coconut oil • 3 tablespoons tapioca flour
400g can diced tomatoes • 500ml *Chicken stock* (see page 14) • 2 bay leaves
1 tablespoon red wine vinegar • 1 quantity *Cauliflower white sauce* (see page 34)
salt and freshly ground black pepper

High in iron, omega-3 fatty acids, B vitamins, zinc and potassium to help strengthen the immune system.

(Be) *Bone enhancing* (A) *Anti-inflammatory* (EP) *Eye protecting*

Dust meat in 3 tablespoons flour. Heat half oil in casserole dish and brown meat all over, adding half the vinegar. Set aside. Add more oil if needed and sauté celery and leeks for 6–8 minutes until starting to soften. Add tomatoes and stock then bring to the boil. Remove and blend with hand-held blender until smooth. Add meat with remaining vinegar and bay leaves and simmer, covered, for 1–2 hours until meat is tender. Serve with white sauce and season.

POULE AU POT

Serves: 4

YOU NEED

1 whole free-range chicken • 1 lemon, sliced • ½ bulb garlic, cut in half

4 thyme sprigs • 1 small handful of flat-leaf parsley

2 litres *Chicken stock* (see page 14) or water • 5 baby spring onions, trimmed

2 carrots, chopped into batons • salt and freshly ground black pepper

Full of vitamin D to help strengthen bones and teeth and vitamin B to boost the immune system.

Hs *Heart support*   **IF** *Infection fighting*   **EP** *Eye protecting*

Stuff chicken with lemon, garlic and herbs. Heat large pan over medium heat and brown chicken on both sides. Cover with stock. Bring to the boil then simmer, covered for 1 hour. Add onion and carrot and simmer for 20–30 minutes until soft. Season, remove from liquid and serve chicken with vegetables and broth on the side.

POT AU FEU

Serves: 4

YOU NEED
4 x grass-fed beef osso bucco • 1kg grass-fed beef brisket

2 bay leaves • stalks of 1 bunch of parsley

1 onion, sliced • 1 bunch of baby carrots, peeled

2 turnips, peeled and quartered • 3 celery sticks, cut into 10cm pieces

salt and freshly ground black pepper

Restores health, boosts joint function and helps to strengthen bones.

I *Immunising* **A** *Anti-inflammatory* **Mm** *Aids memory*

Put all beef into a casserole dish and season well. Add bay leaves and parsley stalks.
Pour in 2.5 litres water and cover with lid. Bring to the boil, then simmer for
2 hours, skimming off foam. Remove bay leaves and parsley stalks and add
remaining ingredients. Simmer until vegetables have softened. Serve.

CAVEMAN BURGER

Serves: 2

YOU NEED

300g grass-fed beef mince • 1 organic egg yolk

1 small onion, cut into rings • 2 garlic cloves • 2–4 outside leaves of iceberg lettuce

½ avocado, peeled, pitted and sliced • 15g flat-leaf parsley

1 tablespoon coconut oil • salt • 1 tablespoon *Paleo tomato sauce* (see page 26)

1 tablespoon *Paleo mayo* (see page 28)

This burger has a low glycaemic index (GI) and is high in protein, potassium, iron and zinc.

BSt *Bone strengthening*　　**E** *Energising*　　**I** *Immunising*

Preheat oven to 180°C/350°F/Gas 4. Pulse parsley, half the onion and garlic in a food processor until finely chopped. Season mince and add parsley mix and yolk. Bring together, divide in half and shape into 2 patties. Heat oil in pan. Cook patties for a few minutes on each side to brown. Place on baking tray and bake for 10–15 minutes. In same pan, cook remaining onions until soft. Put patties in lettuce with onions, avocado and condiments.

GARLIC & CHILLI PRAWNS

Serves: 2

YOU NEED

3–4 tablespoons *Chilli sambal* (see page 24)

300g raw prawns, peeled and deveined • 1 bunch of broccolini or tenderstem

broccoli • ½ lemon, plus extra to garnish • 2 tablespoons sesame oil

1 tablespoon sesame seeds

Prawns are an excellent source of protein, vitamin D, selenium, copper and zinc and can help boost the immune system.

 Bone strengthening   *Anti-ageing*   **Mm** *Aids memory*

Stir chilli sambal through prawns. Cover and chill for 1–2 hours. Heat wok with half the sesame oil over medium heat. Add prawns, turning as they cook for 4–5 minutes. Set aside. Add remaining oil to wok and cook broccolini for 4–5 minutes. Return prawns and heat for 1–2 minutes. Squeeze lemon juice over, sprinkle with sesame seeds and serve with juices from wok.

RIB STEAKS WITH MINTY PEAS

Serves: 2

YOU NEED

2 grass-fed rib steaks • 100g frozen peas

100ml *Chicken stock* (see page 14) • 1 handful of mint leaves, finely chopped

10g organic butter • salt and freshly ground black pepper

Rich in omega fatty acids, protein and vitamin B12 to help in the formation of healthy red blood cells.

I *Immunising*   **Hs** *Heart support*   **Mm** *Aids memory*

Season steak. Heat frying pan over high heat. Fry each steak for 5–6 minutes on either side or to own preference. Heat stock in a pan, add peas and cook for 2–3 minutes. Drain, add mint and butter and stir well. Rest steaks for 4–5 minutes. Serve with peas.

CAULIFLOWER FRIED RICE

Serves: 2

YOU NEED

1 medium cauliflower, broken into florets • 1 rasher of grass-fed bacon, diced

10 raw prawns • 80g peas, fresh or frozen • 1 small onion, diced

2 organic eggs, lightly beaten • 2 teaspoons sesame oil • 2 tablespoons tamari

1 tablespoon *Paleo tomato sauce* (see page 26)

Peas contain fibre and balance blood sugar levels while cauliflower and bacon contain choline to help boost memory and keep the brain healthy.

A *Anti-inflammatory*   **E** *Energising*   **I** *Immunising*

Blitz cauliflower in a food processor until it resembles breadcrumbs. Heat oil in wok over medium-high heat. Sauté onion until soft. Add bacon and cook until beginning to brown and crisp. Add prawns and sauté for 2 minutes. Add cauliflower to wok and stir. Working quickly, make a well in the centre and pour in egg. Slowly move egg through the cauliflower as it cooks from the base of the pan. Mix in remaining ingredients.

PORK & PEARS

Serves: 2

YOU NEED
400g grass-fed pork belly, scored, rinsed and patted dry • 2 pears
juice of ¼ pineapple • 1 flat-leaf parsley sprig • olive oil, for drizzling • salt to taste

Grass-fed pork is full of protein, B vitamins and zinc to boost the immune system while pears are full of fibre to help control blood sugar levels.

BSt *Bone strengthening*   **E** *Energising*   **Hs** *Heart support*

Sprinkle salt over pork. Cover with kitchen paper and chill for 1 hour. Preheat oven to 220°C/425°F/Gas 7. Juice 1 pear and pineapple. Peel and quarter remaining pear. Drizzle oil in roasting dish and place the quartered pears in base. Place pork on top. Roast for 20–25 minutes until skin starts to crackle. Remove and reduce temperature to 160°C/325°F/Gas 3. Pour juice around pork. Roast for 1–1½ hours. Slice pork, garnish with parsley and serve with pears.

BANGERS & SWEET POTATO MASH

Serves: 1

YOU NEED

2 good quality grass-fed pork sausages • 1 sweet potato, peeled and diced

3 garlic cloves, unpeeled • 2 rosemary sprigs • 1 tablespoon butter (optional)

1 tablespoon *Paleo onion jam* (see page 32), optional

1 tablespoon olive oil • salt to taste

Rich in vitamins and minerals and can help to stabilise blood sugar levels.

A *Anti-inflammatory*　　**E** *Energising*　　**Hs** *Heart support*

Preheat oven to 180°C/350°F/Gas 4. Place sweet potatoes, sausages, garlic and rosemary in roasting dish. Drizzle with oil and season. Roast for 15 minutes. Turn sausages and cook for 15 minutes until potatoes are soft and sausages cooked. Discard rosemary. Place sweet potatoes in a bowl, squeeze in roasted garlic, add butter and mash. Place under sausages with onion jam, if using, on top.

MEDITERRANEAN LAMB

Serves: 4

YOU NEED

1kg piece of boned grass-fed lamb (leg or shoulder), cut into rough cubes

1 eggplant, sliced into wedges • 6 roma tomatoes, sliced into rounds

1 red capsicum, sliced • juice of 1 lemon • 10g flat-leaf parsley, roughly chopped

1 tablespoon cumin seeds • 2 tablespoons olive oil • 1 teaspoon salt

Low in calories, high in protein and iron from the lamb and packed with antioxidants from the tomatoes and red capsicum.

HR *Hair repairing* **Hs** *Heart support* **MR** *Muscle repairing*

Preheat oven to 160°C/325°F/Gas 3. Place lamb, eggplant, capsicum and parsley in baking dish. Drizzle with oil and sprinkle with salt and cumin seeds. Toss to combine. Top with tomato slices and squeeze lemon juice over. Pour in 125ml water, cover with foil and bake for 1½ hours. Uncover, increase temperature to 190°C/375°F/Gas 5 and cook for 20–25 minutes until slightly reduced and browned on top.

ZUCCHINI BOLOGNESE

Serves: 2

YOU NEED

600g grass-fed beef mince • 2 medium zucchini

40ml red wine vinegar • 140g tomato purée

400g can diced tomatoes • 80g shallots, diced • 30g diced garlic

60ml olive oil • salt to taste • chopped parsley, to garnish (optional)

Zucchini contains lots of fibre to aid digestion, stabilise blood sugar levels and prevent constipation while grass-fed beef contains lots of iron.

I *Immunising* **E** *Energising* **A** *Anti-inflammatory*

Heat 2 tablespoons oil in a pan over medium heat. Sauté shallots and garlic until softened. Add vinegar and mince. Season and cook for 6–8 minutes until browned. Add remaining oil, a little more salt and tomato purée and stir until mince is coated. Add diced tomatoes and 125ml water. Bring to the boil. Simmer for 30 minutes until thick. Grate or use spiraliser to make noodles from zucchini. Serve bolognese over noodles garnished with parsley.

PALEO LASAGNE

Serves: 4–6

YOU NEED

2 eggplants, sliced • 1 quantity *Bolognese mince* (see page 132)

1 quantity *Cauliflower white sauce* (see page 34)

30g salt • coconut oil, for oiling

High in fibre, protein, B vitamins and magnesium to help with fatigue.

Hs *Heart support* **E** *Energising* **I** *Immunising*

Spread eggplant out on kitchen paper. Sprinkle with salt. Leave for 30 minutes.
Preheat oven to 200°C/400°F/Gas 6. Oil baking dish. Put a layer of eggplant in
base of dish then a thin layer of white sauce. Top with a thick layer of mince and
continue to layer with remaining ingredients, finishing with white sauce. Bake for
30–40 minutes until golden brown.

SEAFOOD CHOWDER

Serves: 2

YOU NEED

200g chopped leeks • 200g chopped cauliflower • 150g chopped parsnip

1 onion, chopped • 1 small bunch of dill

500ml *Chicken stock* (see page 14) • 400g mixed fish and seafood

3 tablespoons olive oil • fresh lemon, to taste • a pinch of sea salt

Seafood is packed with essential vitamins and minerals including omega-3 fatty acids, which boost energy and help keep the heart healthy.

BB *Brain boosting* **A** *Anti-inflammatory* **EP** *Eye protecting*

Heat 2 tablespoons oil in lidded pan over medium heat. Sauté onions and other vegetables with salt. Add stock and most of dill, cover and bring to the boil. Simmer for 30 minutes. Remove dill and strain vegetables, reserving liquid. Blitz vegetables in food processor, adding some reserved liquid until smooth. Fry fish and seafood mix in remaining oil until just coloured. Pour purée over seafood and simmer for 4–5 minutes until seafood is cooked. Garnish with remaining dill and lemon juice.

VEGETABLE CURRY

Serves: 2

YOU NEED

80g snow peas, trimmed and cut in half • ¼ cauliflower, cut into florets

2–3 tablespoons green curry paste, depending on taste • 400g can coconut milk

3 ripe tomatoes, diced • 2 tablespoons coconut oil

1 small onion, sliced • 2 teaspoons fish sauce

juice of ½ lime • coriander leaves, to garnish

Lactose free and loaded with fibre, minerals and vitamins A, C, K and B to help boost the immune system.

A *Anti-inflammatory* **D** *Aids digestion* **E** *Energising*

Heat oil in wok over medium heat, add curry paste and onion and cook for 4–5 minutes until onion is soft and paste fragrant. Add cauliflower and sauté for 1 minute. Pour in coconut milk and add tomatoes. Simmer for 7–8 minutes. Add snow peas and fish sauce and mix. Remove from heat, squeeze lime juice over and garnish with coriander.

139

MUSHROOM & LEEK SOUP

Serves: 2

YOU NEED

150g button mushrooms, sliced • 1 medium leek, roughly chopped

80g cauliflower chopped • 1 rosemary sprig • ½ onion, diced

2 garlic cloves • 400ml *Chicken stock* (see page 14)

1 tablespoon coconut or olive oil

Leeks can help to support the cardiovascular system while mushrooms are packed with calcium and potassium to help strengthen bones.

I *Immunising*　　**E** *Energising*　　**CR** *Cholesterol reducing*

Heat oil in lidded pan over medium heat. Add rosemary and vegetables and cook for 5 minutes until browned. Season and add stock. Cook, covered, for 1 hour, stirring occasionally until vegetables are soft. Cool. Remove rosemary. Blend with hand-held blender, adding more stock if needed.

PUMPKIN GNOCCHI

Serves: 2

YOU NEED

250g butternut pumpkin, peeled, deseeded and cubed

½ sweet potato (200g), peeled and cubed • 100g coconut flour

200g tapioca flour • 1 organic egg, slightly beaten

100g mushrooms, sliced • 30g baby spinach • 1 tablespoon butter

coconut oil, for oiling • salt to taste

Low in calories, full of fibre and packed with potassium to help
lower blood pressure and reduce the risk of strokes.

 BSt *Bone strengthening*   **A** *Anti-inflammatory*   **HP** *Heart protection*

Preheat oven to 180°C/350°F/Gas 4. Oil roasting dish. Put pumpkin and sweet
potato into dish. Season with salt and roast for 20–25 minutes until soft. Cool. Blitz
vegetables, coconut flour, half tapioca flour and egg in food processor until smooth.
Spread remaining tapioca flour over surface. Break dough into small pieces and
roll each into 3cm tubes. Cut into smaller pieces. Cook gnocchi in boiling water for
2–3 minutes until they rise to top. Drain. Heat butter in pan. Cook mushrooms and
spinach for 5 minutes until soft. Mix in gnocchi.

WILD FISH WITH SALSA VERDE

Serves: 2

YOU NEED

2 x 160g wild white fish fillets (bream, snapper), skin left on

60g cherry tomatoes, quartered • 1 small handful of basil leaves

1 small handful of mint leaves • 2 anchovies in olive oil

1 garlic clove • juice of 1 lemon • 20g activated macadamia nuts

salt and freshly ground black pepper • 2 tablespoons coconut oil

Helps to lower blood pressure as fish is packed with healthy omega-3 fatty acids and tomatoes contain potassium.

 **Mm** *Aids memory*   **I** *Immunising*   **HP** *Heart protection*

Heat oil in pan over medium-high heat. Season fish on both sides and place in pan, skin side down. Cook for 4–5 minutes until skin is crispy and golden. Turn and cook for 4–5 minutes. Whizz basil, mint, anchovies, garlic, nuts and lemon juice in a food processer until finely chopped. Mix with tomatoes. Serve on top of fish.

SWEETS

Strictly speaking you won't need to include these sweet treats in your Paleo lifestyle – eliminating sugar and processed foods will change the way you crave this kind of food. However, these recipes are Paleo friendly and will be the perfect treat for visitors or to give you a little extra variety in your diet.

Nutty raspberry friand bites
Paleo chocolate brownie • Nut energy bars
Salted caramel energy balls
Roasted peach crumble

NUTTY RASPBERRY FRIAND BITES

Makes: 12 mini muffins

YOU NEED

75g organic butter or coconut oil, melted, plus extra for greasing

4 tablespoons maple syrup • 2 organic eggs, separated • 75g ground hazelnuts

30g coconut flour • 1 teaspoon baking powder • 50g frozen or fresh raspberries

Contains lauric acid from the coconut to help boost the immune system and strengthen bones, while raspberries can help stabilise blood sugar levels.

AA *Anti-ageing*　　**D** *Aids digestion*　　**M** *Metabolism boosting*

Preheat oven to 160°C/325°F/Gas 3. Use melted butter or oil to grease a 12-hole mini muffin tin. Combine flour, hazelnuts and baking powder. Add egg yolks and melted oil or butter and mix. Beat egg whites to soft peaks, then while mixer is on slowly pour maple syrup into whites and beat until stiff. Fold egg whites into flour, one-third at a time. Place a heaped teaspoon of batter into each muffin hole. Bake for 15 minutes. Cool and put raspberry on top of each.

PALEO CHOCOLATE BROWNIE

Makes: 16 squares

YOU NEED

1 zucchini, grated • 45g raw cacao powder • 4 organic eggs, lightly beaten
60ml coconut oil, plus extra for oiling • 8 Medjool dates, pitted and roughly
chopped • 80ml maple syrup • 70g ground almonds
2 tablespoons coconut flour • 1 teaspoon baking powder

Cacao is good for the brain and may help to improve memory while dates
are packed with minerals to help strengthen bones.

I *Immunising*   **E** *Energising*   **HP** *Heart protection*

Preheat oven to 200°C/400°F/Gas 6. Grease 20cm square tin. Combine dates, syrup
and oil in a pan and heat gently for 3–5 minutes. Stir and break up dates. Combine
flours, cacao and zucchini. Add eggs and date mixture and stir until well combined.
Pour into tin and bake for 20–25 minutes, or until set. Cool in tin, then turn out
and cut into squares.

NUT ENERGY BARS

Makes: 10 bars

YOU NEED

75g activated cashew nuts • 80g activated almonds • 100g activated macadamia nuts

30g chia seeds • 30g sesame seeds • 125ml honey

25g goji berries • ½ teaspoon sea salt

Nuts and seeds are high in fibre and are packed with healthy omega-3
fatty acids to help lower cholesterol.

BSt *Bone strengthening*   **S** *Skin repairing*   **HP** *Heart protection*

Preheat oven to 180°C/350°F/Gas 4. Line 20cm baking tin with baking paper. Pulse
nuts and goji berries in a food processor until finely chopped. Tip into a bowl and
add seeds and salt. Heat honey gently to thin then stir through nut mix. Pour into
tin and press down with back of spoon. Bake for 15–20 minutes. Cool for 30 minutes
before removing from tin. Once cooled completely, cut into bars.

SALTED CARAMEL ENERGY BALLS

Makes: 12–15 balls

YOU NEED

200g desiccated coconut • 12 Medjool dates, pitted

1 teaspoon natural vanilla extract • 1 teaspoon sea salt flakes

2 tablespoons sesame seeds, for coating

Coconut and dates can help boost energy and stabilise blood sugar levels.

Blitz coconut, dates, vanilla and salt in a food processor until chopped
and well combined. Remove and roll into small balls, about 30g each.
Coat in sesame seeds.

ROASTED PEACH CRUMBLE

Serves 4

YOU NEED

2 ripe peaches, halved • 40g activated pecan nuts

30g desiccated coconut • 1½ tablespoons sunflower seeds

2 tablespoons coconut flour • 40g organic butter or coconut oil

1 tablespoon maple syrup (optional) • ½ teaspoon ground cinnamon

High in fibre to help the digestive system and prevent constipation.

AA *Anti-ageing*   **S** *Skin repairing*   **EP** *Eye protecting*

Preheat oven to 200°C/400°F/Gas 6. Combine pecans with flour, coconut and pumpkin seeds. Roughly rub butter into flour mix with fingertips. Chill. Place peaches in a baking dish, sprinkle with cinnamon and drizzle with maple syrup, if using. Roast for 20 minutes until softened. Spoon 2 tablespoons of flour mix onto each peach half then bake for 10 minutes until golden brown.

INDEX

Published in Australia and New Zealand in 2016
by Hachette Australia
(an imprint of Hachette Australia Pty Limited)
Level 17, 207 Kent Street, Sydney NSW 2000
www.hachette.com.au

10 9 8 7 6 5 4 3 2 1

Cataloguing-in-Publication data is available from
the National Library of Australia.

978 0 7336 3601 1 (pbk.)

Acknowledgements

We would like to thank everybody involved in the conception and making of this book. Elisa, it was wonderful to have the opportunity to work with you for the first time, thank you. To Catie, Alice and Kathy, once again – a great team. To Kath and Jodi, assistant extraordinaires, and to our family for their continued support and help day to day.
x Amelia and Alex

Publisher: Catie Ziller   Authors: Amelia Wasiliev & Alex Wasiliev
Designer & illustrator: Alice Chadwick   Photographer: Elisa Watson
Food Stylist: Amelia Wasiliev   Editor: Kathy Steer

Colour reproduction by Splitting Image
Printed in China by Toppan Leefung Printing Limited